FACIAL RECOGNITION
and Other Security Tech

Co-published by agreement between Shi Tu Hui and World Book, Inc.

Shi Tu Hui
Room 1807, Block 1,
#3 West Dawang Road
Chaoyang District, Beijing 100025
P.R. China

World Book, Inc.
180 North LaSalle Street
Suite 900
Chicago, Illinois 60601
USA

Copyright © 2024. All rights reserved. This volume may not be reproduced in whole or in part in any form without prior written permission from the publishers.

WORLD BOOK and the GLOBE DEVICE are registered trademarks or trademarks of World Book, Inc.

Library of Congress Cataloging-in-Publication Data for this volume has been applied for.

Cool Tech (set, hardcover)
ISBN: 978-0-7166-5479-7

Facial Recognition and Other Security Tech
ISBN: 978-0-7166-5482-7 (hardcover)
ISBN: 978-0-7166-5494-0 (softcover)
ISBN: 978-0-7166-5488-9 (e-book)

Written by Alex Woolf

STAFF

VP, Editorial: Tom Evans
Manager, New Product: Nicholas Kilzer
Curriculum Designer: Caroline Davidson
Proofreader: Nathalie Strassheim
Coordinator, Design Development & Production: Brenda Tropinski
Digital Asset Specialist: Rosalia Bledsoe

Developed with World Book by
White-Thomson Publishing LTD
www.wtpub.co.uk

ACKNOWLEDGMENTS

Cover	© Yuri A, PeopleImages.com/Shutterstock
5-15	© Shutterstock
16-17	© Lucky Step/Shutterstock; © Charles D. Winters, Science Photo Library; © Steklo/Shutterstock; © Metamor Works/Shutterstock
18-25	© Shutterstock
26-27	Chao-Yang Lu, University of Science and Technology of China; © Pattyariya/Shutterstock; Cousin Avi/Shutterstock; © Production Perig/Shutterstock
28-29	© Shutterstock
30-31	© Marija Crow, Shutterstock; © Lals Stock/Shutterstock; © Ildogesto/Shutterstock; © Philippe Psaila, Science Photo Library
32-33	© Pixel-Shot/Shutterstock; © Angyalosi Beata, Shutterstock; © Victor Habbick Visions/Science Photo Library; © Aquarius Studio/Shutterstock
34-45	© Shutterstock

CONTENTS

Acknowledgments 2

Glossary 4

Introduction 5

1. Facial Recognition 6
2. Biometrics 12
3. Cybersecurity 20
4. Surveillance 28
5. Access Control 36

Resources 46

Index 48

There is a glossary of terms on the first page. Terms defined in the glossary are in boldface type **that looks like this** on their first appearance in the book.

GLOSSARY

artificial intelligence (AI) the ability of a computer system to process information in a manner similar to human thought or to exhibit humanlike behavior.

authenticate to prove or show something to be true, genuine, or valid.

cloud in computing, this is all of the things you can access remotely over the internet. When something is in the cloud, it means it's stored on internet servers instead of on your computer.

composite made up of different parts.

computer virus a type of software that places a copy of itself within another computer program and can spread to other software after the infected application is run.

credentials a set of unique identifiers, such as a username and password, that enables a user to verify identity in order to log in or enter a building.

cybercrime criminal activities carried out by means of computers or the internet.

database a collection of related records or information stored on a computer and organized to make any part of it accessible.

digital includes all types of electronic equipment and applications that use information in the form of numeric code.

drone an uncrewed aerial vehicle. Most drones are piloted by remote control.

encrypted information converted into secret code that hides the information's true meaning.

false positive a result that indicates that a certain condition is present when it actually is not.

fraud an intentional untruth or a dishonest scheme used to take deliberate and unfair advantage of another person or group of people.

machine learning the use of computer systems that are able to learn and adapt to new situations without following prewritten instructions.

prime number factor prime numbers are numbers that have only 2 factors: 1 and themselves. Factors of a number are numbers that, when multiplied together, give the original number. For example, the first 5 prime numbers are 2, 3, 5, 7, and 11.

random number a number chosen by chance from a set of numbers.

remote sensing any technique used to gather information about an object from afar without actually touching it.

software application a computer program designed to carry out a specific task.

virtual reality (VR) an artificial, three-dimensional computer environment. A VR experience is typically viewed through a headset. It replaces what a person normally sees and hears with computer-generated images and sounds.

INTRODUCTION

Imagine a world where your identity can be confirmed by your heartbeat, your walking style, or your voice. Bug-sized camera **drones** fly around watching for signs of criminal activity. Robot security guards patrol buildings on the lookout for intruders. And when you meet someone new, you can call up their entire history on your smart contact lenses. An advanced computer program will sift through it and tell you whether he or she can be trusted. The technology that could make this world a reality already exists. Whether we want to live there is another question.

Security has always been important and necessary for us. Historically, people protected themselves with thick walls, locked doors, and guards. Today, we use more sophisticated technology to keep ourselves, our families, and our property safe. Instead of human guards, we use security cameras. In this **digital** age, we use both physical walls and computer firewalls to protect our secrets. In the past, criminals could hide behind a mask of anonymity. That's harder today, thanks to facial recognition and other biometric technologies. This book looks at the many ways security tech is transforming the way we protect ourselves.

1 FACIAL RECOGNITION

TURNING A FACE INTO NUMBERS

With so many people alive in this world, it's hard to believe that every face is unique. How many combinations of two eyes, a nose, and a mouth can there be? Yet, when analyzed mathematically and turned into a string of numbers, our faces are as individual as our fingerprints. Facial recognition is used to establish an individual's identity in photos, videos, and in real life.

The police and security services use this technology to scan faces in crowds and try to match them to a photo of someone they are searching for, such as a missing person or a suspected criminal. Technology can be used to identify individuals at a crime scene or establish an alibi (prove someone was elsewhere at the time a crime was committed). Facial recognition is used at airports to ensure passengers match their passport photos. Many of us use it to unlock our phones or access banking apps. It's a convenient way to keep our devices and our money secure.

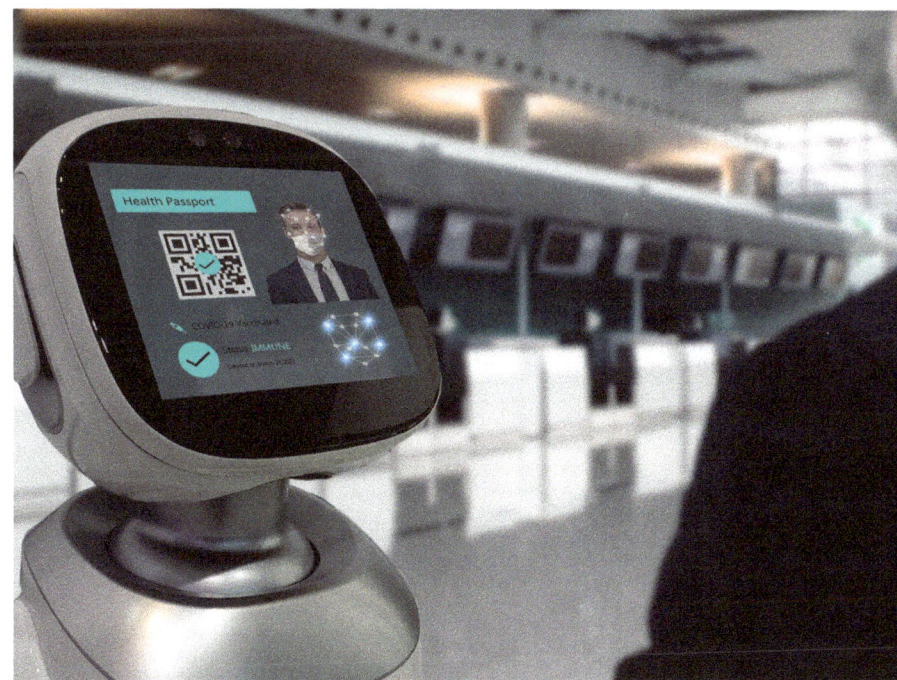

HOW FACIAL RECOGNITION WORKS

Facial recognition **authenticates** a person's identity by comparing two photos of their face or a live image of their face with a photo. It does this by using **artificial intelligence (AI)** to capture and analyze a person's face and turn it into digital data, which can then be compared to the digital data of other faces. Facial recognition is quick and easy to use. It can be used remotely, and it doesn't involve physical contact like taking fingerprints does.

Our unique faces. A person's face has its own unique geometry. Key identifying factors include the distance between the eyes, the distance from forehead to chin, and the shape of cheekbones, lips, and ears. All these factors can be mapped by a computer that converts the data into a mathematical code known as a faceprint, which is as unique as your thumbprint or DNA. This can be compared to millions of other faceprints in a **database.** If one or more matches are found, they are given similarity scores that indicate their likeness to the original faceprint.

The learning algorithm. An AI program is called an algorithm—a set of rules written in code a computer can understand. The algorithm behind facial recognition is called a convolutional neural network (CNN). The CNN is fed an image of a face and assigns a weight (a level of importance) to different parts, such as the nose or the mouth. The more images it is fed, the better it gets at assigning these weights. This is how a CNN learns to recognize faces. In 2014, the most accurate CNN algorithm had an error rate of 4.1 percent when matching faces. By 2020, this number had fallen to 0.08 percent. The algorithms can recognize faces even when superficial changes, such as adding a beard or eyeglasses, are made. Today, a facial recognition technology called Facewatch can identify people even if they are wearing a mask covering their lower face. The algorithm works by analyzing unique characteristics around the eyes.

Biases. Facial recognition algorithms are more effective at identifying certain groups, such as white men compared to other groups, such as women and people of color. The latter groups aren't as well represented in the dataset used to train the algorithm. This can lead to **false positives** (incorrect matches) and the risk of innocent people being charged with crimes. If facial recognition is to become a trusted technology, it will have to improve to eliminate such biases.

Ethical concerns. Is facial recognition a violation of our human rights? If we post a selfie on social media, we usually don't mind if it is viewed by others. But that doesn't mean we consent to it being turned into a faceprint and added to a police database. And what about images of ourselves captured without our permission from security cameras? Many people believe that the use of facial recognition technology without consent is an invasion of privacy.

FACIAL EMOTION RECOGNITION (FER)

While facial recognition is used to identify people, facial emotion recognition (FER) is about identifying emotions. As humans, we are highly skilled at reading people's emotions. We don't need to hear someone speak to know they are thrilled, shocked, amused, or annoyed. Computers have traditionally found this more difficult. But with FER technology, computers are getting better at analyzing human emotions through lip, eye, nose, and eyebrow movements.

Facial expressions can be classified in terms of basic emotions, such as joy, sadness, surprise, anger, disgust, and fear. Then there are compound (mixed) emotions, such as happily sad, happily surprised, sadly angry, and angrily disgusted. Some expressions do not reveal an emotion but a state of mind, such as boredom or tiredness. As FER algorithms improve, they will be able to detect more complex emotions and states of mind.

How does it work? To start, skilled human observers examine slow-motion video footage of facial movements, then code and label each one with an emotion. This data is fed into a CNN. Movie footage is often a useful source of emotional expressions.

The programmers start with the most basic emotions before moving on to more complex ones. In this way, the CNN builds up a database of facial expressions and their meanings. The bigger the database, the better the results: A thousand images

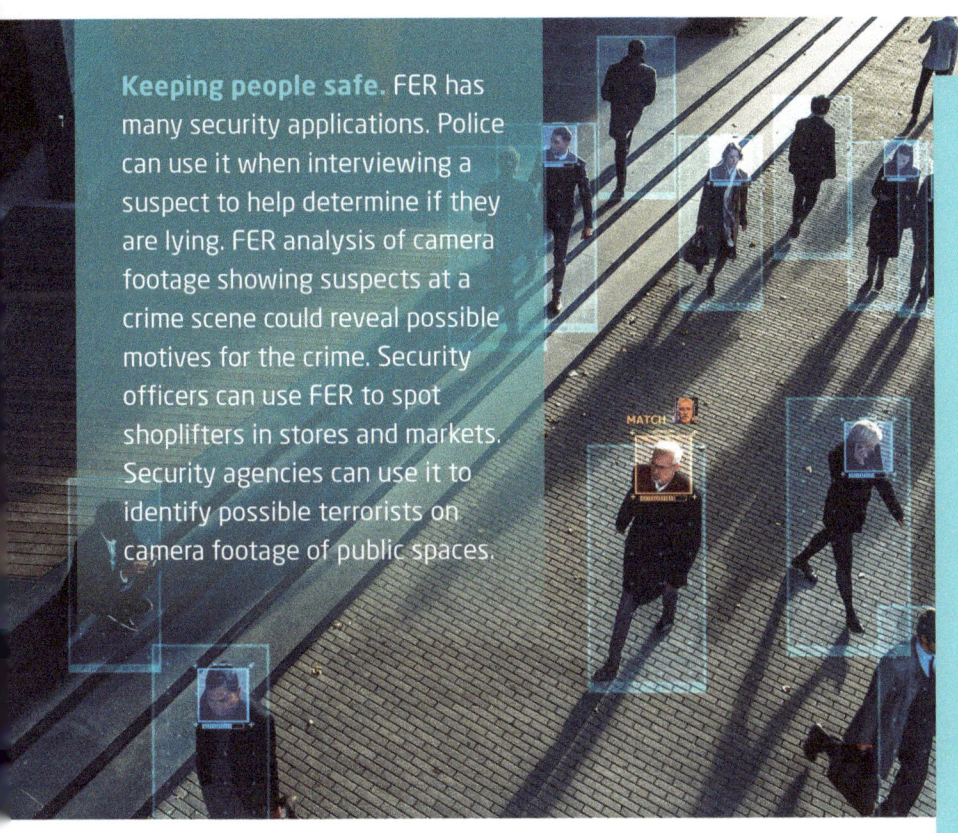

Keeping people safe. FER has many security applications. Police can use it when interviewing a suspect to help determine if they are lying. FER analysis of camera footage showing suspects at a crime scene could reveal possible motives for the crime. Security officers can use FER to spot shoplifters in stores and markets. Security agencies can use it to identify possible terrorists on camera footage of public spaces.

How accurate is FER? FER is far from foolproof. The meaning of a facial expression can vary among individuals, depending on gender, age, and ethnicity. Facial expressions can be subtle and highly dependent on context. Some emotions do not reveal themselves on a person's face, and some people are adept at not showing their feelings. Camera angles and poor lighting conditions can mask parts of the face. Even if FER accurately detects an emotion, it cannot explain what caused it. For all these reasons, FER can be misleading and should be treated with caution. Nevertheless, it may be useful as part of a range of tools used by security services when trying to identify suspects.

of happy people will give the algorithm a better understanding of what a happy person looks like than 50 images would. The technology company Affectiva has one of the largest facial emotion databases in the world, with over 7.5 million faces from 87 countries.

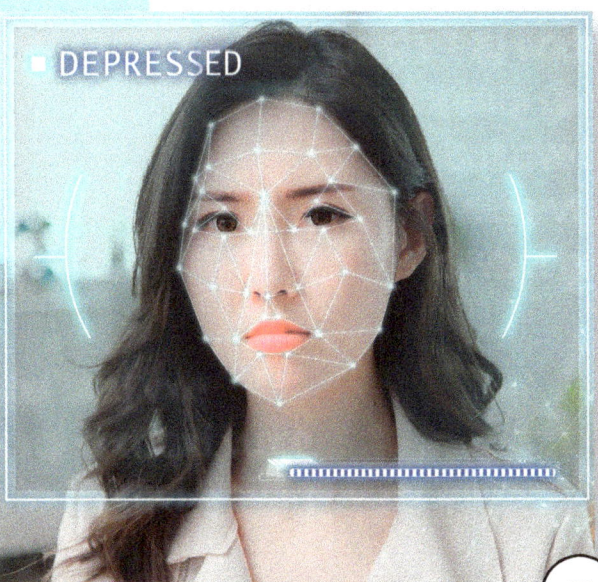

2 BIOMETRICS

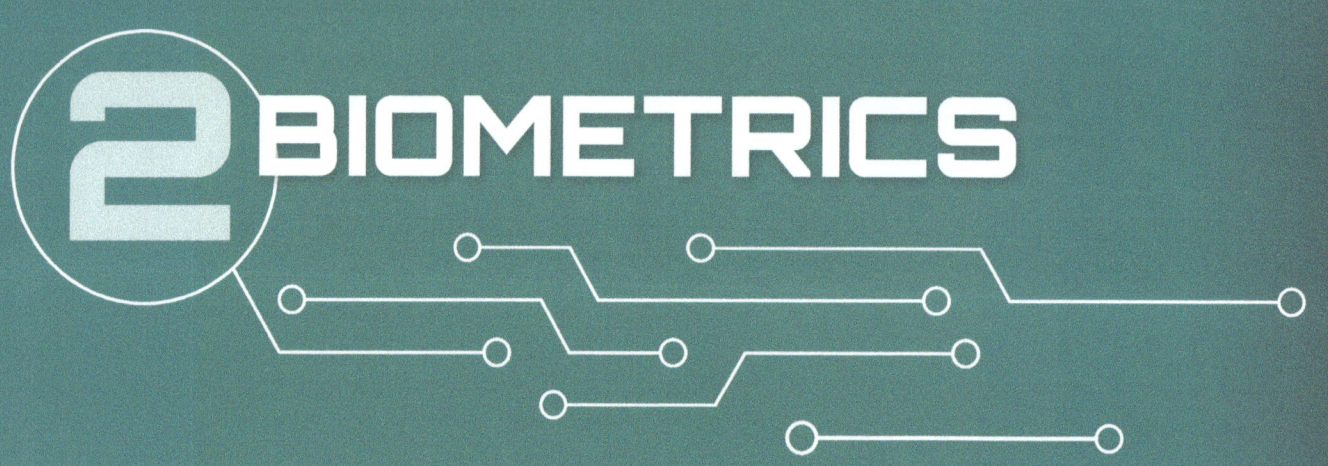

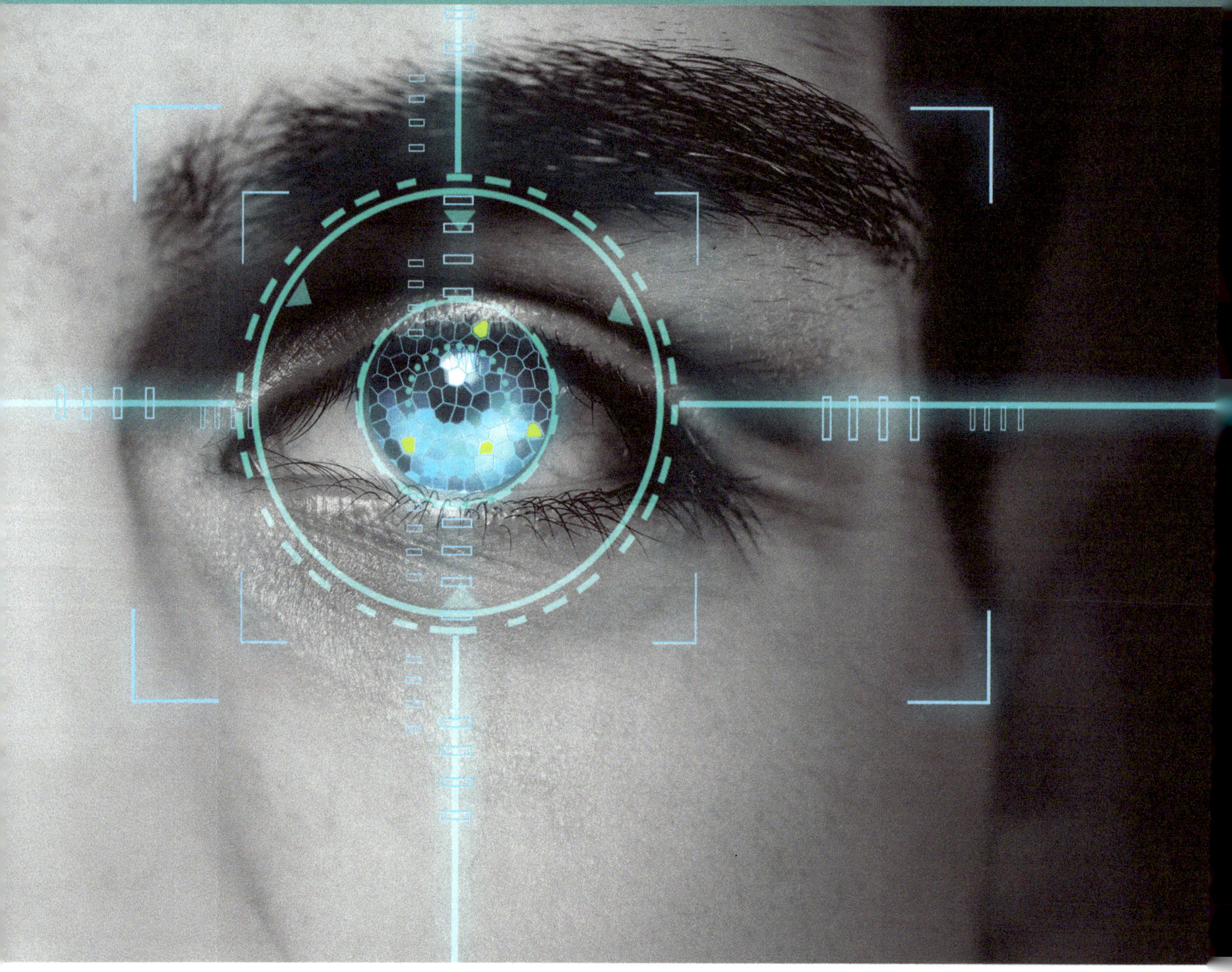

OUR UNIQUE IDENTIFIERS

Many parts of your body are unique and fixed (unchanging) for your entire life, making them useful as a means of identification. Biometrics are characteristics that can be used to identify individuals. We have already looked at one form of biometrics—facial recognition—but there are many more. Physical features that can be used as biometrics include fingerprints, the retina and iris of the eye, ear shape, vein patterns in hands, heartbeat, and your voice.

Biometrics are not limited to our physical features; they can also include the ways we behave. Behavioral biometrics include our gait (walking style), keystroke dynamics (typing style), word preferences, purchasing habits, and gestures. These are just as unique as our body parts.

Biometrics are useful because, unlike keys or passwords, they are hard to steal, copy, or lose. We increasingly use biometrics to identify ourselves to our devices. They are also used at airports and other borders to identify travelers, and by law enforcement officers to track and catch criminals.

PHYSICAL BIOMETRICS

Physical biometrics are a convenient and efficient way of identifying ourselves. The process is quick and involves little effort by the user. It's also fairly failsafe as our physical traits mostly stay the same throughout our lives. Our bodies may age, but our irises, fingerprints, and the vein patterns in our hands do not change. But biometric algorithms struggle with wrinkles and other facial changes associated with aging.

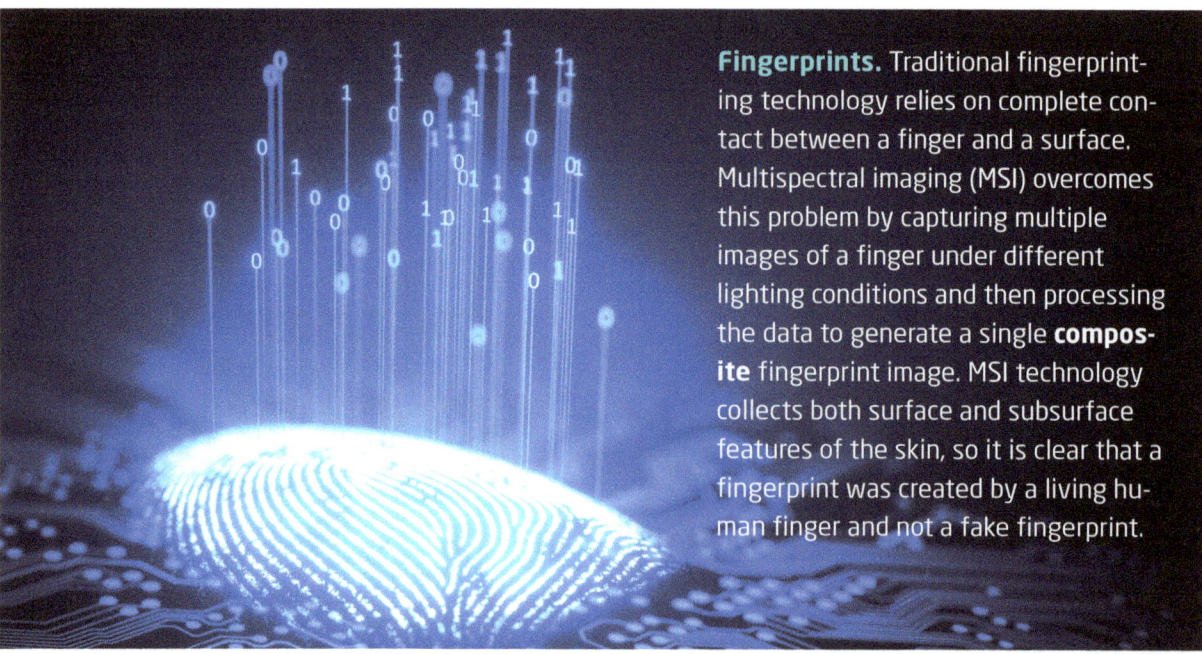

Fingerprints. Traditional fingerprinting technology relies on complete contact between a finger and a surface. Multispectral imaging (MSI) overcomes this problem by capturing multiple images of a finger under different lighting conditions and then processing the data to generate a single **composite** fingerprint image. MSI technology collects both surface and subsurface features of the skin, so it is clear that a fingerprint was created by a living human finger and not a fake fingerprint.

Iris recognition. The iris—the colored portion of the eye—is made up of complex, intricate features. Iris recognition technology analyzes 240 of these features and encodes them in a mathematical formula. Everyone's iris is unique: There is less than a 1 in 10 billion chance that two irises share even 30 percent similarity. Iris recognition is used to identify crime suspects, combat **fraud,** and for border security. No contact is required, and it is very quick. Computers can check an iris against databases containing hundreds of millions of scans in a matter of seconds. However, iris recognition has drawbacks in criminal investigations. Unlike fingerprints, irises leave no trace at a crime scene. And unlike the voice and face, they are hard to identify from recordings.

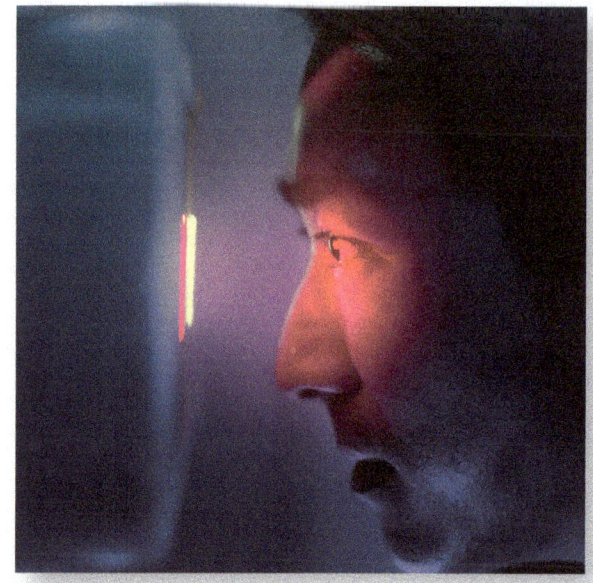

Heartbeat. We all produce a distinctive heartbeat, based on the shape and size of our heart, the arrangement of heart valves, and the pressures they produce. A **remote sensing** device called a laser doppler vibrometer can detect a heartbeat at a distance of up to 650 feet (200 meters). However, the target must be standing still and wearing no more than light clothing, and there must be a clear line of sight between the device and the target. Heartbeat biometric identification could be used to unlock a smartphone or to allow a person to enter secure locations.

Body odor recognition. Human bodies emit a complex range of odors based on factors such as genetics (characteristics inherited from our parents), environment, diet, health, and living habits. Electronic nose-like sensors can capture and analyze body odors to create a unique smell profile that can be used for identification. The algorithm can be taught to filter out temporary odors such as perfumes. Most people are likely to object to body odor recognition as an invasion of privacy, which could limit how it is used.

VOICE BIOMETRICS

Voice biometrics technology turns the unique characteristics of the human voice into a form of identification. The sounds we make are determined by our anatomy, including the size and shape of our vocal cords, voice box, mouth, and tongue. Each of these body parts is unique, as is the way we use them, which is why human voices sound different.

How does it work? A voice can be scanned to produce a wavelike pattern called a spectrogram. An algorithm analyzes the spectrogram and turns it into a mathematical model called a voiceprint. Voiceprints can be stored and compared to other voiceprints as a means of identification. Voice biometric technology can be used by banks, corporations, and law enforcement agencies to check the identity of a caller, or it can be used to ensure that only designated individuals can communicate with certain devices.

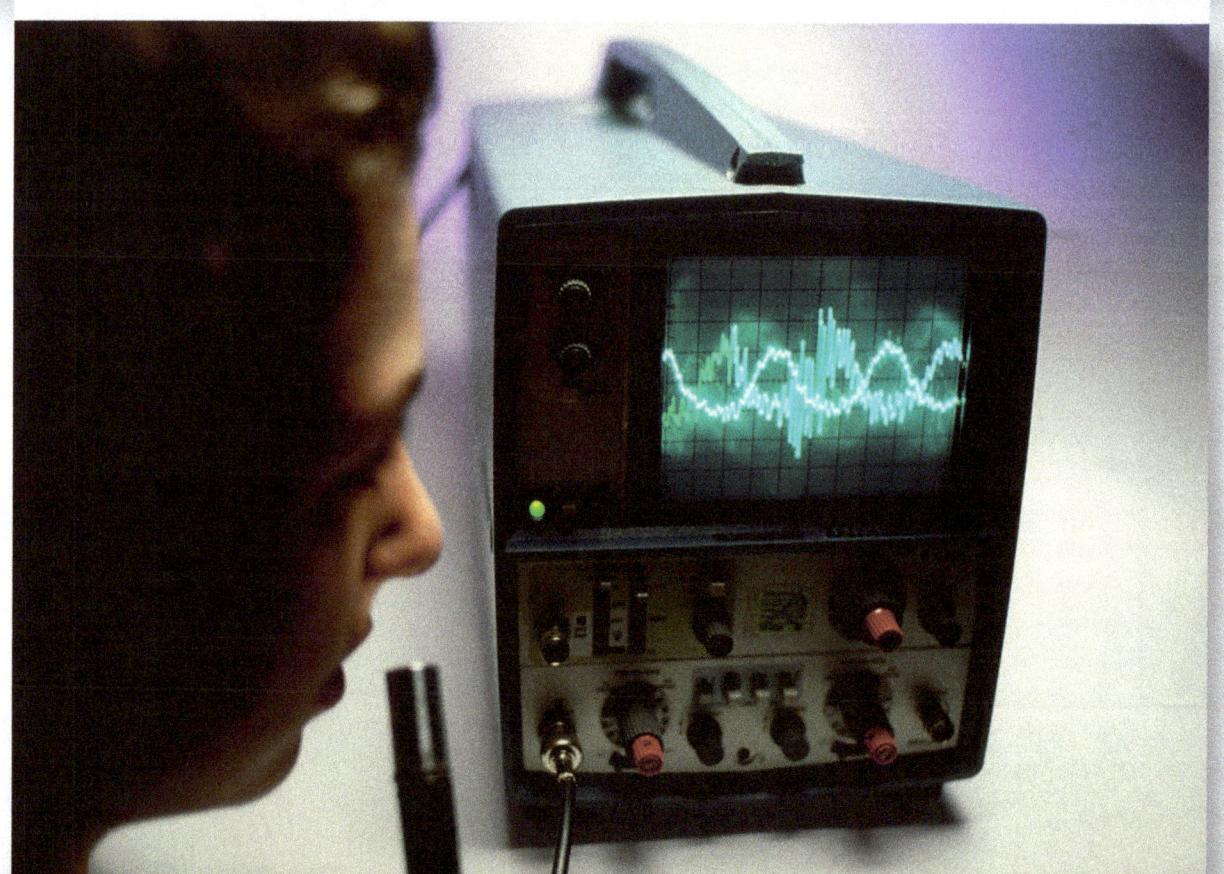

Visualizing the speaker. Voice biometric technology is not only used to identify a speaker, but it can also help create a picture of that speaker. AI algorithms analyze the depth and tone of the voice, the words spoken, the language, accent, and emotion. This enables the algorithm to estimate the speaker's age, gender, height, geographic origin, personality, and mood. The AI may also identify behavioral traits, such as whether a speaker smokes cigarettes. The algorithm can even attempt a reconstruction of a person's face based on the way facial bones shape the voice.

Voice cloning. Criminals can use AI to clone (imitate) a person's voice, by feeding an algorithm a sample of that voice. They may clone the voice of a person's friend or relative to trick that person into sending money. Voice biometric algorithms can also be trained to detect cloned voices to help prevent such crimes. They do this by analyzing subtle speech patterns, such as mouth noises, pauses, sentence length, and vocabulary—traits that are very hard to clone.

The future. Voice biometrics are constantly improving as algorithms learn to extract accurate voiceprints from background noise, illness-affected voices, or faint or disguised recordings. A new voice biometric system called Phonexia allows users to search for and identify individual speakers, keywords, or topics across a large set of audio recordings in multiple languages. Phonexia can run in the background of a telephone call, continually verifying that the speaker is who they claim to be.

BEHAVIORAL BIOMETRICS

Behavioral biometrics focuses on the unique actions of people while they are online. They are used by organizations such as banks to confirm a customer's identity. While physical biometrics are normally used for one-time identification, behavioral biometrics can provide continuous proof that an individual is who they claim to be. Certain behavioral traits are extremely hard to imitate, making this form of authentication highly secure.

Online behavior. We all have our own unique way of interacting with networked devices. This includes our typing style or speed, how hard we press the keys, the way we move a computer mouse, and the websites we click on. This data can be analyzed by AI algorithms to establish patterns of behavior. The next time we attempt to log into a website, the algorithm will assess whether our behavior matches past behavior. We never behave the same way from visit to visit, but the algorithm will assign us a score based on behavioral similarity. If the score is below a certain threshold, it will alert the organization to possible fraud.

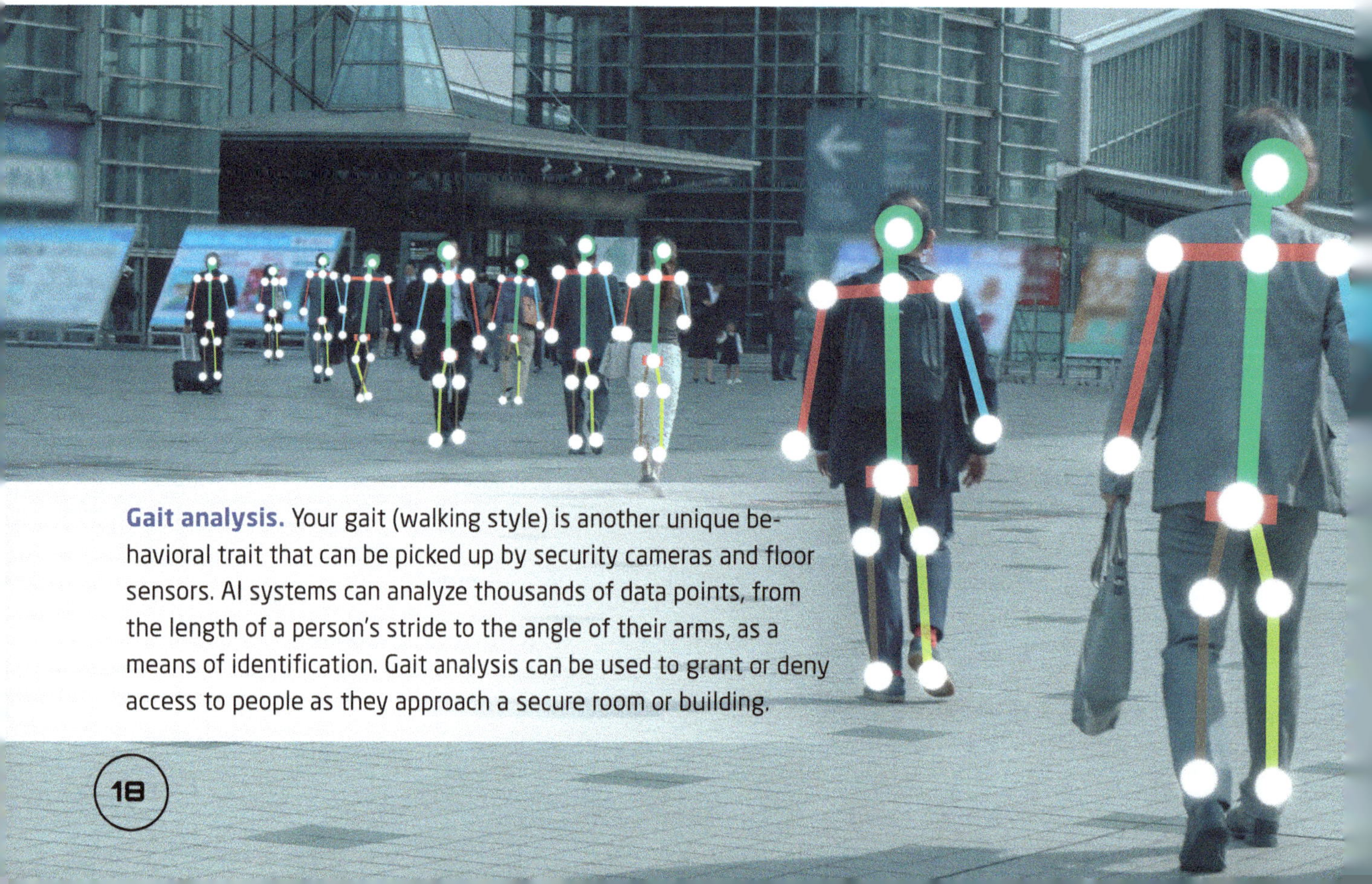

Gait analysis. Your gait (walking style) is another unique behavioral trait that can be picked up by security cameras and floor sensors. AI systems can analyze thousands of data points, from the length of a person's stride to the angle of their arms, as a means of identification. Gait analysis can be used to grant or deny access to people as they approach a secure room or building.

Preferences. We can also be identified through our preferences. This could include preferences for certain words when speaking or writing; the way we use our phones and credit cards; or how, when, and where we shop, and what we buy. For example, you may usually purchase peanut butter and pickles together. Uncharacteristic shopping activity using your credit card detected by AI could trigger an alert to your bank.

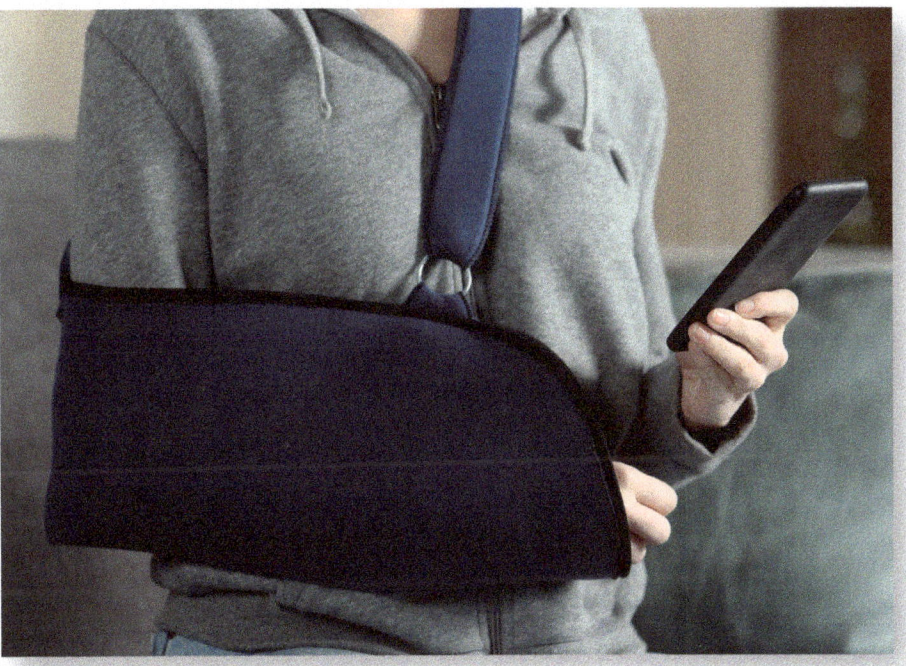

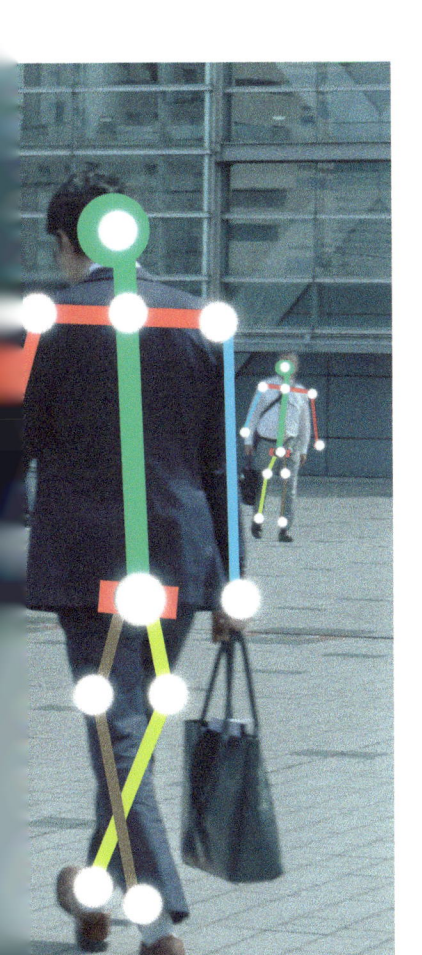

Pros and cons. Behavioral biometrics provides governments, banks, and businesses with an extra layer of security that allows them to monitor users continually, so they can identify fraudsters who happen to get through standard security barriers. Behavioral biometrics can be collected unobtrusively without interrupting the user's activity. They are also very hard to imitate.

The problem with behavioral biometric algorithms is that they must capture and analyze a large amount of data from individuals to accurately profile their typical behavior. Many people view this as an invasion of privacy. Human behavior can also change depending on such factors as weather, season, fatigue, stress, injury, illness, or aging. Effective behavioral biometric models need built-in flexibility to adapt to normal changes in the way we act.

3 CYBERSECURITY

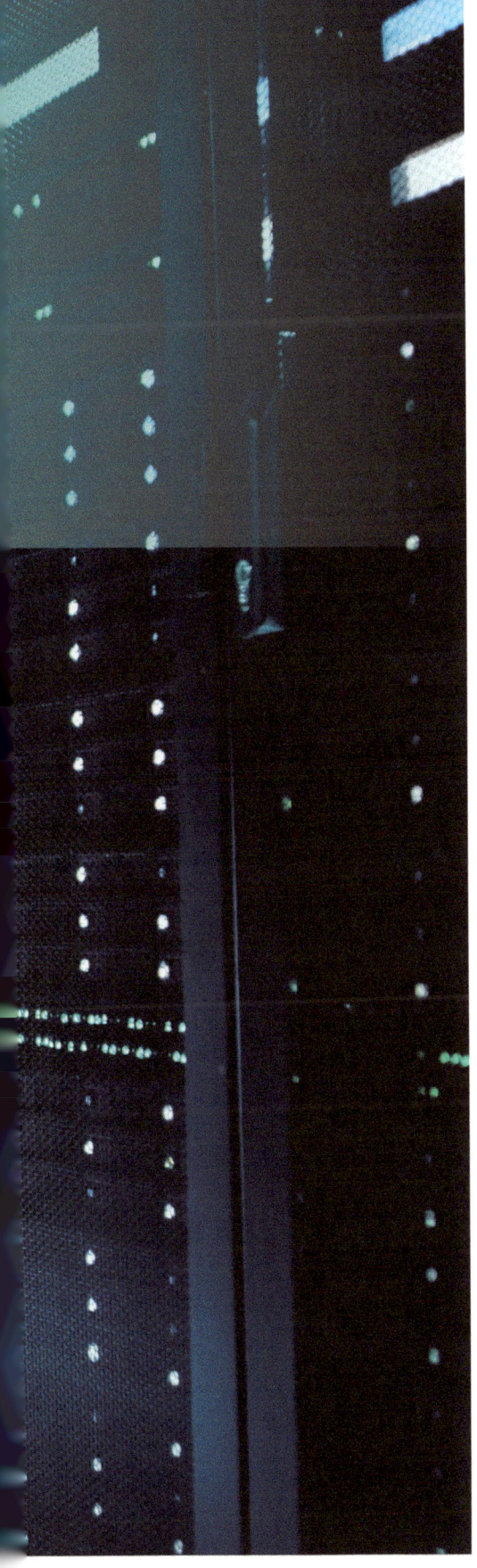

PROTECTING OUR DATA

Our electronic data is at risk from cybercriminals who hack into computer systems. Their aim may be to damage or destroy a business, access sensitive information, or steal customers' personal data or credit card details. **Cybercrime** costs businesses billions of dollars and loss of customer trust every year. Cybersecurity is the practice of protecting computer systems from cybercriminals. Businesses must, first of all, protect their computer network—the servers, the data stored on them, and the personal computers connected to the servers. Second, they must protect the **software applications** running on their computers.

Today, cybercrime is on the rise, helped by recent trends. For example, many people are choosing to work from home rather than at a company office. These remote workers may not always follow the rules to keep their data secure. Another trend is the rise of cloud-based servers. Companies find it cheap and convenient to store their data in the **cloud,** but this can be another point of vulnerability. Companies must ensure that data stored in the cloud, or transferred to and from the cloud, is **encrypted.** We live in an age of increasing connectivity, where devices from kitchen appliances to thermostats are linked to the internet. This so-called "Internet of Things" may offer more opportunities for cybercrime in the future.

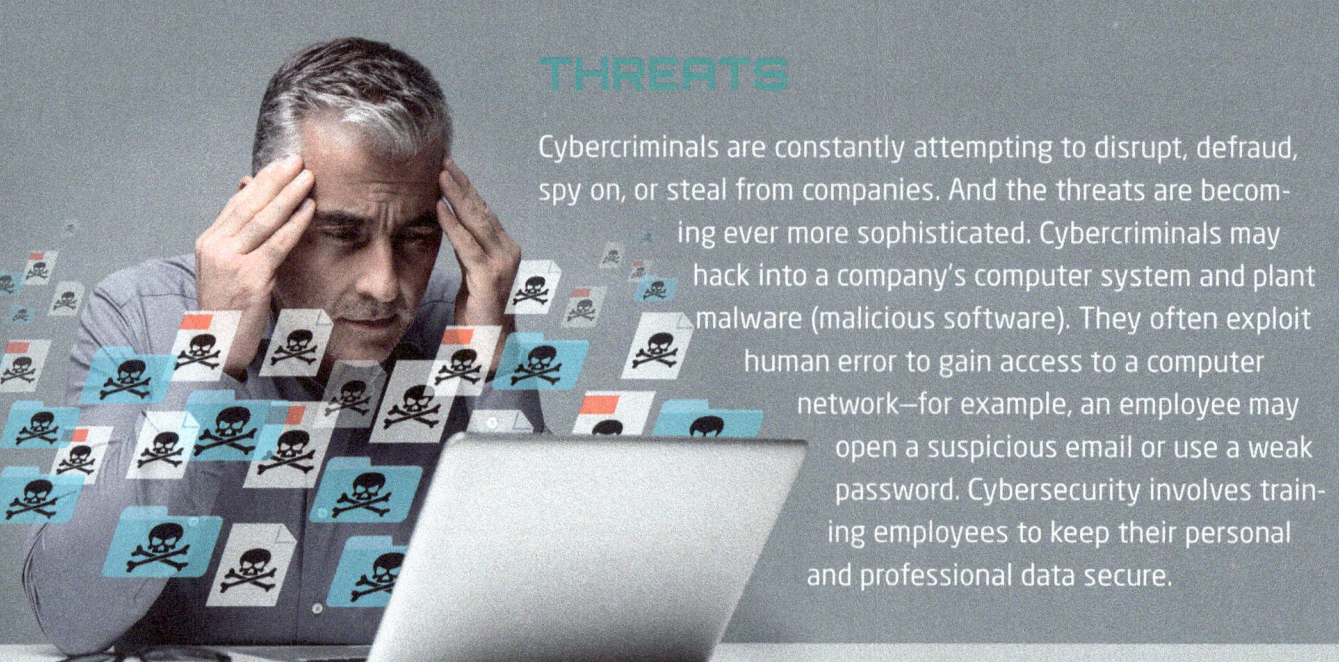

THREATS

Cybercriminals are constantly attempting to disrupt, defraud, spy on, or steal from companies. And the threats are becoming ever more sophisticated. Cybercriminals may hack into a company's computer system and plant malware (malicious software). They often exploit human error to gain access to a computer network—for example, an employee may open a suspicious email or use a weak password. Cybersecurity involves training employees to keep their personal and professional data secure.

Malware is any file or code designed to disrupt a computer or computer network. Malware can copy, change, or delete information from a computer network. It can crash websites and cause immense damage to businesses. Malware can take the form of a **computer virus** or a worm—a piece of code that can copy itself to other computers in a network. A Trojan horse is a type of malware that disguises itself as a normal computer program. Spyware secretly gathers information about a user, and a wiper is a type of malware that erases the data of an infected computer.

Botnet. Bots are software applications that carry out automated tasks on the internet. Most perform useful functions such as communicating with users or carrying out internet searches. But some are used for malicious purposes. A botnet is a network of computers infected by millions of bots under the control of a single attacker. Botnets can execute large-scale coordinated attacks, such as sending malware via spam emails to thousands of people. They can overwhelm a computer network by bombarding it with requests, putting it out of action. This is known as a distributed denial-of-service (DDoS) attack. During a botnet attack, the attacker can adapt to changing circumstances and respond to countermeasures in real time. This makes the botnet attack difficult to defeat.

Ransomware is one of the biggest cyber threats facing organizations today, costing businesses billions of dollars a year. A ransomware attack usually starts with an innocent user opening an email attachment or following a link to a fake website. This allows the attacker to install malware onto their computer system. The malware denies users access to their files, databases, or apps by encrypting their data. The attacker then demands payment of a ransom before restoring access. Ransomware is designed to spread across a network and can thus quickly paralyze a business or organization.

Phishing. Cybercriminals don't always use malware to gain access to computer networks. Sometimes they simply send an email or text or make a telephone call to lure individuals into providing sensitive data. They pose as someone from a legitimate institution, such as the target's bank, and ask for their credit card details and passwords as a means of verifying their identity. This form of cybercrime is known as phishing.

METHODS OF PROTECTION

Companies and organizations are in a race to protect their networks from increasingly sophisticated cyberattacks. One obvious step is to regularly back up (record) and encrypt their data. Another is to ensure that only authorized users can access their network by requiring multiple forms of authentication, including biometrics. Some organizations may go further and use AI algorithms to continually check for suspicious user activity based on behavioral biometrics.

Firewall. This is a digital barrier erected by companies and organizations between their private computer network and the internet. Firewalls are software applications that monitor and filter incoming and outgoing computer traffic and keep dangerous traffic out. The latest firewalls do not wait passively for an attack to occur. They use algorithms to constantly check the network for vulnerabilities before they are breached. Firewall algorithms can learn from past breaches to improve their detection capabilities and react more quickly to future attacks. Some are designed to prevent DDoS attacks by watching for abnormal levels of traffic or traffic with known attack signatures.

Antivirus software. If a piece of malware manages to breach a firewall, the next line of defense is antivirus software. This is software loaded onto individual computers that detects malicious code and either quarantines it (isolates it, so it cannot contaminate other parts of the computer) or deletes it. The latest antivirus products update automatically to protect against ever-evolving threats.

Artificial intelligence. AI has transformed cybersecurity. Traditional cybersecurity systems cannot keep pace with the variety of malware and phishing attacks. **Machine learning** algorithms continually improve their performance by drawing on past experiences. They use pattern recognition to detect even the smallest abnormalities in traffic through the network that might indicate the presence of malware. AI programs can use natural language processing to trawl the internet for the latest articles and studies on cyber threats, so that they are prepared for new forms of attack.

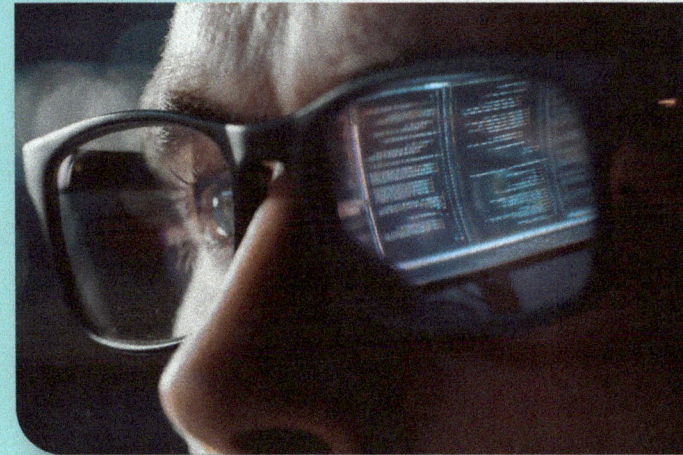

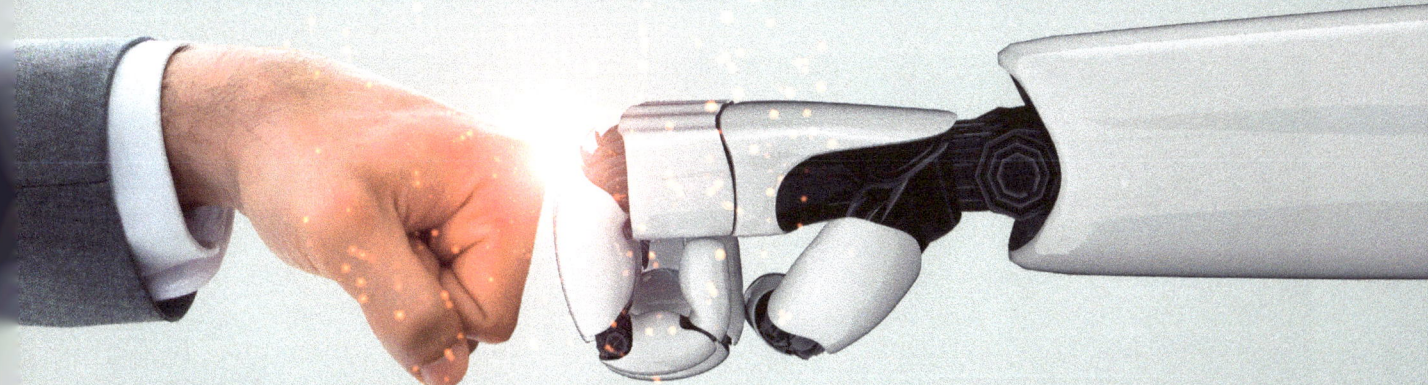

Battling the bots. Much of today's internet traffic is made up of bots, and some of them can be malicious. Traditional AI tools use rule-based methods to protect against bad bots. These methods may block bots from certain countries or data centers known to host bad bots. The latest machine learning tools use more sophisticated algorithms. By analyzing historical data, they can learn the patterns of good bot behavior and block activity that does not conform to these patterns.

CYBERSECURITY AND QUANTUM COMPUTING

A quantum computer is a computer that makes use of quantum mechanics (the motions and interactions of subatomic particles) to store information and make calculations. This allows a quantum computer to perform many calculations simultaneously, making it much faster than a conventional computer. The emergence of quantum computers is set to transform cybersecurity in both positive and negative ways.

Jiuzhang 2.0, a quantum computer developed at the University of Science and Technology of China

Encryption. Computerized data is kept secure from cybercriminals by encryption (converting it into a code). Computer encryption is based on **random numbers.** Algorithms known as pseudo-random number generators provide these numbers. However, they are not truly random because they are generated from particular mathematical formulas. Although it would be extremely difficult, those can be decoded by a computer. Such companies as Quantum Dice are developing quantum random number generators that produce truly random numbers for use in encryption.

Quantum key distribution (QKD). People within an organization often want to share data or exchange messages securely with no possibility of eavesdropping. This can be done by sharing cryptographic keys—strings of data that an algorithm uses to transform code into ordinary text or vice versa. QKD is a secure communication method based on quantum mechanics, which enables two people to produce a shared random secret key known only to themselves. QKD can even alert people to the presence of a spy.

Detecting and defeating malware. AI is getting better at detecting and blocking malware attacks, but machine learning models can only improve by being fed enormous volumes of data—and that uses vast amounts of energy. The emerging field of quantum machine learning could yield effective cybersecurity algorithms more quickly using less energy and at a much lower cost.

Decryption. The development of quantum computing is not entirely good news for cybersecurity. Many of today's businesses and security agencies rely on an encryption system called RSA to encrypt their data. RSA relies on the fact that it is extremely difficult to calculate the **prime number factors** of a very large number. It would take a conventional computer trillions of years to make such a calculation. However, a powerful quantum computer could crack the RSA algorithm in seconds. The world's biggest quantum computer in 2023 is not nearly powerful enough to accomplish this feat. But IBM and Google have plans to build much more powerful quantum computers. Businesses and organizations may soon need a more secure encryption algorithm for their data.

4 SURVEILLANCE

NEW WAYS OF WATCHING

As a society, we are more watched than ever before. Security cameras and sensors are observing our every move in the physical world. Online, our computers and smartphones are collecting our personal data—including who we talk to, where we go, what we buy, our internet browsing history, and what we post on social media.

Such surveillance brings benefits to all of us in terms of greater security—it is harder for criminals and terrorists to operate when public activity is being so closely tracked. Workplace surveillance can benefit employers by allowing them to track the activities of their staff. Businesses can benefit from access to the purchasing behavior of consumers, because it helps them target advertising toward their most likely customers.

On the other hand, many people see this surveillance as an invasion of privacy. As individuals, we don't know what personal data is being collected, how securely it is stored, or how it is used. What happens if our personal data falls into the wrong hands or is used against us?

Despite these concerns, we are likely to face more, not less, surveillance in the future. With advances in cellular network coverage, AI, and the Internet of Things, surveillance technology is set to become ever more interconnected, intelligent, and omnipresent.

CAMERAS

Today, there are over a billion surveillance cameras installed worldwide. And the technology is improving all the time. Soon, the grainy, black-and-white images of traditional security cameras will be replaced by sharper, color video, as the cost of ultra-high-definition displays comes down. Cameras are also becoming smaller, smarter, and more mobile, so that they can be placed anywhere.

3D motion detection cameras use radar to detect the distance of an object, providing more precise detection of motion within a set area. Users can select areas they want the camera to monitor to avoid false alarms from birds, trees, and traffic. Another feature uses AI to calculate in real time the path being taken by someone outside the property from an aerial perspective.

AI cameras. The latest surveillance cameras use AI to analyze the scenes they are recording and identify vehicles from their license plates and people using facial recognition or other biometrics. AI Guardman, developed by a Japanese technology company, uses AI to detect shoplifting in stores and violent activity in crowds. It analyzes body, hand, and facial points in camera images to calculate people's poses in real time. The AI matches these to pre-learned poses used by people acting in suspicious or violent ways.

Drones. Cameras mounted on drones may in the future be used to patrol property and live stream images to users. AI software will allow drones to fly autonomously, using sensors to avoid obstacles.

Fly on the wall. Scientists are developing bug-sized, autonomous (self-driving) drones that could soon be used for surveillance. These micro aerial vehicles (MAV's) may be shaped like hummingbirds, dragonflies, or bees, propelling themselves by flapping their wings at high speed. They can buzz along streets or down corridors, maneuver through tight spaces, hover, and fly in any direction—all while recording video.

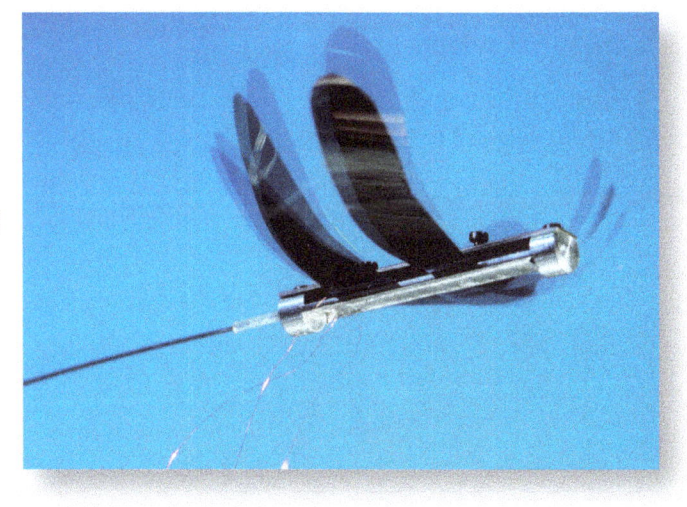

Israel Aerospace Industries has built a butterfly-shaped drone controlled remotely by a pilot. Wearing a **virtual reality** (VR) helmet, the pilot can see what the drone sees in real time. The AeroVironment Nano Hummingbird has a wingspan of just 6.3 inches (16 centimeters) and propels itself by flapping its wings. It can fly in any direction or simply hover with a maximum flight time of 11 minutes.

One technological hurdle faced by designers of MAV's is how to power them. Batteries are too heavy. Some are powered by tiny solar cells. RoboFly, designed by a team at the University of Washington, gets its power from a laser beam directed at a photovoltaic cell on the MAV, which converts the light to electricity. Future MAV's may be able to harvest electricity from wires and other sources as they pass by them.

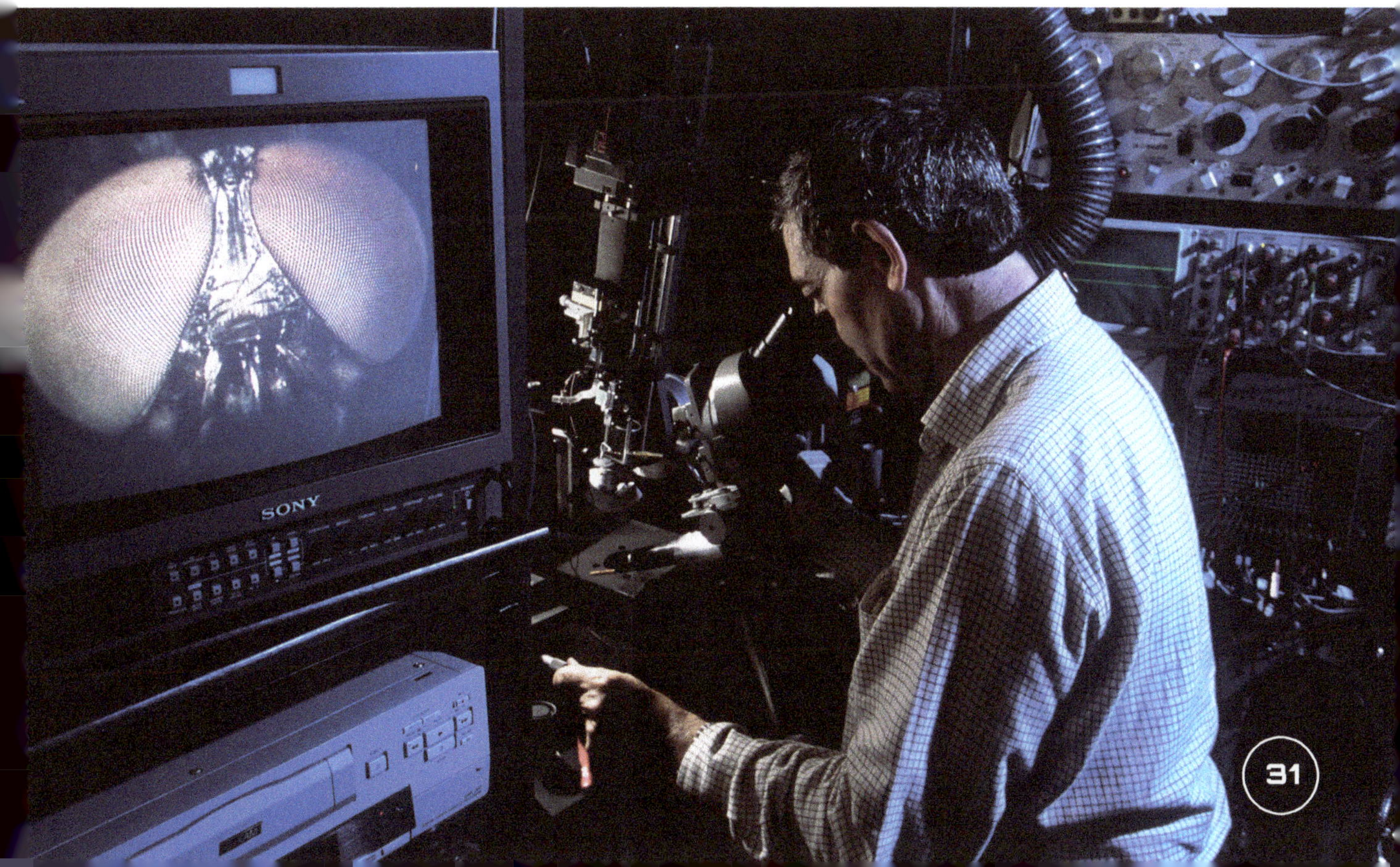

SENSORS

Surveillance doesn't just involve cameras using visible light. Increasingly, other forms of detection are being employed to pick up such signals of human presence as motion, heat, and sound. These systems are less noticeable than cameras and also less invasive of people's privacy. This kind of surveillance is often used to detect intruders rather than to identify them.

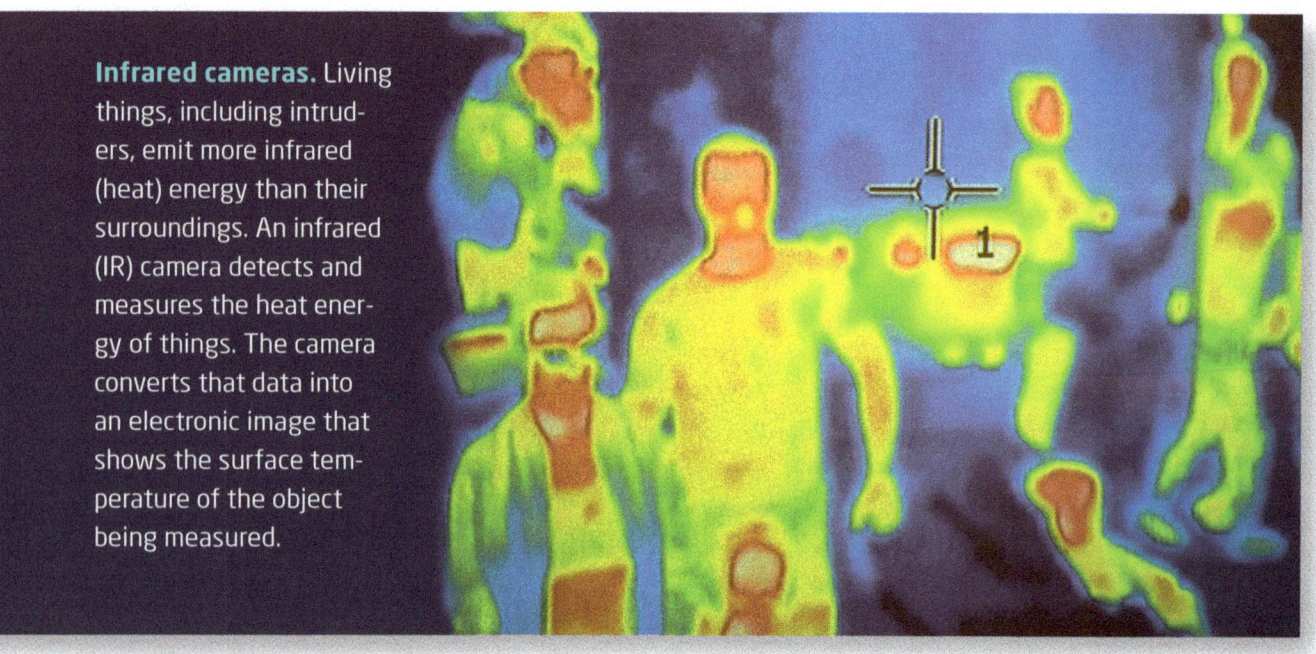

Infrared cameras. Living things, including intruders, emit more infrared (heat) energy than their surroundings. An infrared (IR) camera detects and measures the heat energy of things. The camera converts that data into an electronic image that shows the surface temperature of the object being measured.

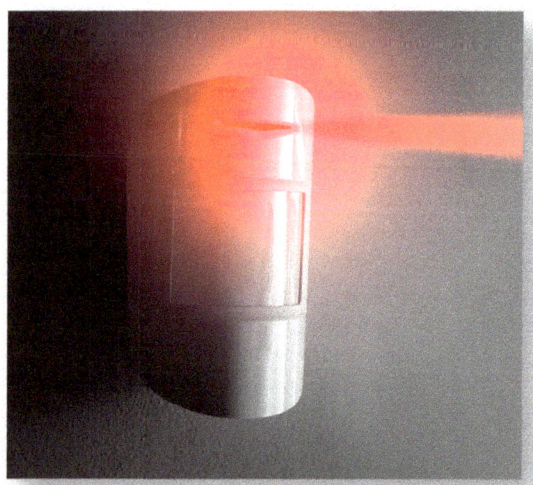

Motion sensors. Infrared can also be used to sense motion. An IR sensor emits and receives infrared radiation. The radiation hits objects nearby and bounces back to the receiver on the device. This allows the device to detect movement and also calculate how far away an object is. Microwave sensors work in a similar way but are more sensitive than IR sensors. This results in more false alarms, but they are better for long-distance detection.

Laser sensors are often used in high-security settings, such as bank vaults and museums. Projectors beam laser light at a detector, and if an intruder steps through the light and the detector no longer senses it, an alarm is triggered.

A tomographic motion detector uses a network of radio transmitters and receivers to detect motion within an area. It works by detecting interruptions in signals between transmitters and receivers. Unlike other forms of motion detection, it does not need line of sight to trigger an alert.

Wi-Fi. A building's Wi-Fi (wireless internet) network can be used to detect human presence and movement from outside a room. As this technology advances, a security system could use Wi-Fi to identify people's position in a room, whether they are sitting or standing, and even track their heartbeat and breathing, giving clues to their emotional state. This could help security guards assess the threat posed by an intruder and possibly distinguish one person from another.

Smart dust is a network of tiny devices, each one the size of a grain of salt, equipped with sensors that continuously record the environment around them, including light, vibrations, temperature, magnetism, and chemicals. The particles, which are suspended in the air like dust, transmit this data using a form of wireless communication called radio frequency identification (RFID) to a central location for processing. They can be used to interact with electronic devices to track the movement of intruders.

NEW TRENDS

Today, we leave a data trail wherever we go. In our homes, our internet-linked devices offer a potential window into our private lives for hackers. Online, our browsing history is tracked by companies hoping to sell us things. In the streets, police are increasing video surveillance, coupled with AI analytics, to help fight crime. Inevitably, this means collecting and analyzing images of millions of innocent people. We need to balance our desire to protect ourselves from crime with our right to privacy. As the power and reach of surveillance technology advances, so does the likelihood that it may be abused. As a society, we need to decide whether we wish to continue along this path or reclaim more of our privacy.

Spies in the home. It is certainly convenient to communicate with our devices through smartphone apps and voice-activated virtual assistants. However, computers, webcams, baby monitors, smart appliances, and even some children's toys can all be hacked. To stay secure, we should turn off microphones and cameras when not in use; avoid giving virtual assistants access to credit card information or personal contact lists; and add extra layers of security, such as voice recognition and passwords, to access our devices.

Police use of AI. Police forces are using AI to analyze surveillance footage and telecommunications interceptions to identify criminal patterns and trends. The aim is to create real-time crime mapping and hopefully predict crimes before they happen.

Surveillance state. The amount of police surveillance is rising, with in-car and body cameras, drone cameras, and smartphone video footage from the public. In the United States, police car cameras can capture and run checks on the license plates of passing vehicles, along with their location and the time they were observed. The information is entered into a database. This can help the police when searching for cars used in crimes. In some states, the data is quickly deleted if it is determined to be noncriminal. But in other states, that data is kept.

ShotSpotter is a noise sensor that detects the sound of gunshots and then sends an alert to the nearest police department. Critics point out that this technology is not accurate and sends police on many false alarms. Others worry that this technology could be used to collect other sounds and even eavesdrop on conversations.

Phone data. Police use Stingray, a sensor that picks up metadata (nonvoice call data) on nearby phones. That could include texts, websites visited, who you called, and how long you called. It is often used to capture phone data from suspected criminals, but it also scoops up data from any people nearby.

5 ACCESS CONTROL

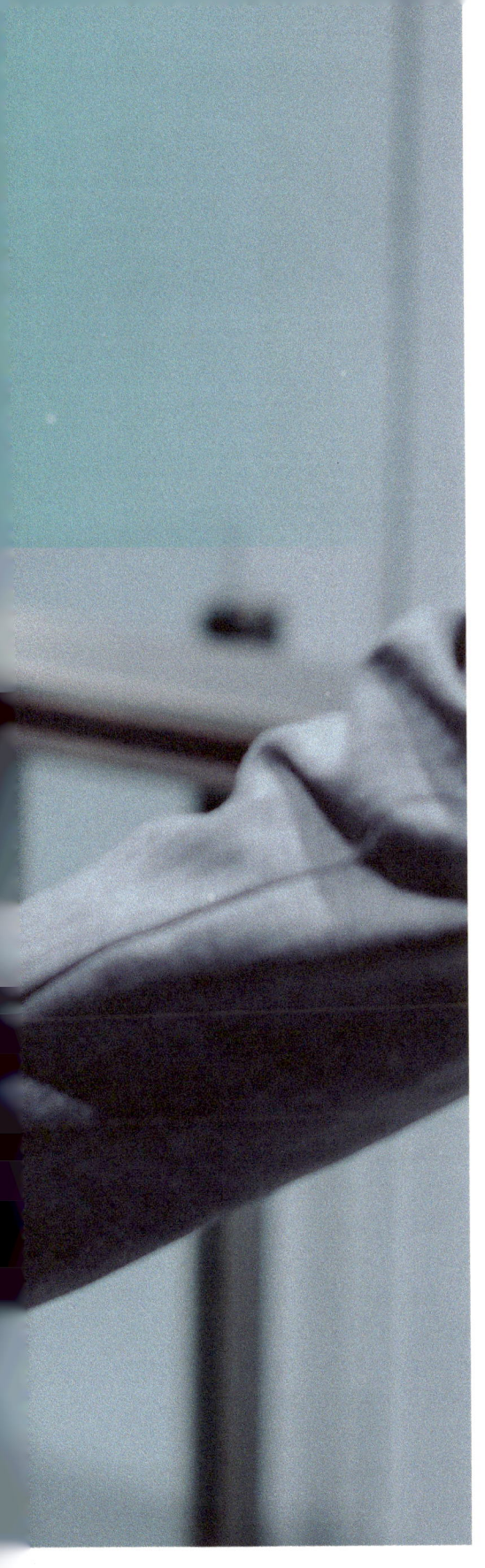

THE RISE OF SMART ENTRY SYSTEMS

Throughout history, people have found it necessary to restrict access to certain places, be they rooms, buildings, or cities. The earliest of all security technologies were developed for access control, including walls, fences, ditches, and bolted doors, later followed by the mechanical technologies of locks and keys. These have worked well for many centuries, but they have their drawbacks. Keys can be copied or stolen, and they leave no record of who used them or when.

Today, we have enhanced or replaced lock-and-key systems with digital technologies. To access restricted spaces, people may have to key in a code, hold a card to a reader, use an app on their smartphone, or present their eye, face, fingerprint, or voice to a scanner. When access is granted or refused, a record of the event is logged on a computer. Any attempt at a forced entry triggers an alert.

In short, entry systems have become smart. Computers and AI are starting to replace human guards and sentries. Where human decisions need to be made on whether or not to let someone in, this can often be done remotely. These trends in access control are likely to continue as we move toward a future of smart buildings, the Internet of Things, and robot security.

HOW WE ENTER BUILDINGS

Many of today's large buildings, such as office buildings, leisure centers, conference halls, and factories, have centralized entry systems. These are made up of several components: an entryway; a computer system that controls who can enter; a keypad or reader where the user can enter a code or present their **credentials;** a locking mechanism; and a request-to-exit device.

Door control. This computer system is the invisible central hub of entry systems in many large buildings. The door controller communicates with and controls every entryway. It has a list of users with access permissions and what their credentials are, and it sends commands to the locking mechanisms to unlock or not unlock as necessary. It keeps records of which users have passed through which entryways and when.

Administrators can program the door controller to, for example, block or restrict access to particular places at particular times or to certain personnel. Door controllers can detect obstructions in entryways or technical issues with a reader, and alert staff to deal with the situation. If there is a security breach, the door controller can institute a lockdown, immediately locking all entryways into the building.

Readers. These devices, mounted on the wall outside entryways, scan or read users' credentials and send this data to the door controller. There are several types of readers. With keypad readers, users are allocated a unique PIN code, a set of numbers that they must key into the reader. This system is less secure than others since PIN codes can be forgotten, stolen, or shared with others.

Keycards and fobs have a magnetic strip or RFID signal that stores their user's credentials, and these are scanned by the reader. The process is very quick, and the system is ideal for entryways with high foot traffic, such as a busy office reception area. However, cards can be lost, shared, or stolen. Biometric readers, which scan fingerprints, irises, faces, or voices, are the most secure form of reader. But biometric readers are also the most expensive.

Intercom systems. Whereas workplaces often use automated digital entry systems, most private residences still rely on traditional locks and keys. However, homeowners can add a layer of security in the form of an intercom system. This can be audio only or audio/video. Intercoms enable two-way communication from the door or gate to the monitor, so users can hear and sometimes also see the visitor before letting them in via a remote unlocking mechanism.

Today, many intercom systems are connected to the internet and can be controlled via a smartphone app. The app sends a notification when someone arrives, and the user can view a real-time video of the visitor. They can speak with them and grant them access if desired. Video recordings of trespassers can be sent to the police.

CONVENIENCE AND SECURITY

People want the experience of entering and exiting buildings to be swift, efficient, convenient, and hygienic. They desire a flexible access control system that allows for changed plans or unusual work conditions. At the same time, they want to feel safe from intruders. These aims can be achieved with touchless systems, multifactor authentication, and advances in cellular technology.

Touchless. Germs can be spread from shared surfaces. With touchless access control systems, people can enter or exit a building with no need to touch door handles or keypads. With a touchless system, you can unlock a door using an app on your phone, presenting your face or eye to a reader, or even by waving your hand in front of a reader. With this last method, your hand triggers an authorization request from your phone to the reader via Bluetooth. This works even if your phone is in your pocket. Once the door controller has verified your credentials, it sends a signal that activates an automatic door-opening mechanism powered by an electric motor. Automatic doors open by sliding, swinging, folding, or revolving.

Multifactor authentication (MFA) is a new trend in security systems in which users must provide more than one method of verification to confirm their identity. When used in access control, MFA provides a building with an important additional layer of security. The most common MFA combinations are a password or keycard together with a voice, fingerprint, or iris.

Cellular technology. Smartphones and other cellular devices, such as smartwatches, are fast replacing keycards as methods of access control. The user places the device near a door reader, and the device transmits the user's credentials using Bluetooth or Wi-Fi technology. This has many advantages. It means less plastic for us to carry around. At event venues, people can use one app to make reservations and obtain access with a digital ID. At work, people can schedule meetings and reserve and access rooms, again with a single app. Cellular devices are more secure than keycards and passwords, and credentials are less easily stolen. Administrators can use the management dashboard of the app to block or restrict access to unwanted visitors.

Remote access. With more people working from home, being able to remotely control access to a site can be very useful for letting in contractors, couriers, or employees. Administrators can activate a remote lockdown in emergencies using an app on their cellular device. Remote access is especially helpful when managing multiple sites.

FUTURE TRENDS

Traditionally, buildings with access control systems require a server, or central computer, based inside the building to manage this function. Staff are needed to maintain and update the server and run its software applications. This is all changing as access control systems are increasingly moved to the cloud. These are a lot easier and cheaper to manage with no need for on-site servers or maintenance staff.

The Cloud. Cloud servers are located remotely in data centers all over the world and are accessed over the internet. A cloud-based system offers all the benefits of on-site access control at a much lower cost, and it can be used across multiple sites. This is particularly useful for large companies and organizations because it gives a small team of administrators centralized access control over several offices. Employees and visitors can be issued digital passes for access to particular rooms at particular times. If there is an intruder or technical fault, the system will send an alert along with a live video feed to administrators' smartphones. Cloud-based systems can provide detailed, real-time activity reports, so administrators know who is in the building at all times. If something goes wrong, cloud-based systems offer remote troubleshooting and diagnostic tools, lessening the need for on-site maintenance. Software upgrades are performed instantly, reducing downtime.

Data analytics. Access control systems collect enormous amounts of data about who uses buildings and when. Such companies as Hakimo have developed AI software that can analyze this data to help with security. For example, Hakimo's AI can expose cases of impossible travel, such as when the same keycard is used in two locations within a short period. The AI can also integrate cybersecurity data with access control data. So if someone in a company's San Francisco office logs into their email at the same time as their keycard is used to enter the New York office, the algorithm can spot this anomaly and send out an alert.

Smart buildings are buildings where all the facilities, including lighting, heating, and plumbing, are linked up to and coordinated by a central computer. Tiny sensors around the building feed real-time data to this computer, telling it how the building is being used, so that it can run the building efficiently and not waste energy. These sensors can also feed back data about human activity, and an AI can analyze this for signs of anomalous or inappropriate behavior—such as attempted unauthorized entry to parts of the building or unauthorized use of computers.

DEALING WITH INTRUDERS

Sometimes, despite all efforts at access control, intruders succeed in breaking in. The final element of any access control system involves dealing with physical breaches of a site or building. Human security guards are usually employed for this. Today, those guards are assisted by the latest technology.

Geofencing. A geofence is a virtual wall that can mark the boundary of a building or site. Geofencing is a technology that uses RFID, Wi-Fi, GPS, or cellular data to detect when a cellular device enters or exits the geofence. It is increasingly used by security guards as a means of detecting intruders. Geofencing can show precisely which part of the boundary has been breached, and send out an alert if the detected device is unauthorized. Geofences can vary in shape or size to protect anything from a room to a secure area in a war zone. They can be extended high into the sky to detect unauthorized drones. A vehicle can be connected to a geofence, so an alert is issued if a car is driven out of a geofenced area.

Wearables. Today, security guards can wear smart jackets with a panic button to connect them with emergency services, a video camera for intruder identification, and GPS for tracking. The jackets also have an internet connection, which they can use to monitor worker schedules so they know if someone is authorized to be on site. They can pair their jacket with a smart helmet and goggles offering them night vision, a voice-activated camera, radio communication, and even an augmented-reality image projection system that can digitally tag items within their field of vision.

Robot security. Autonomous Security Robots (ASR's) are being used to patrol high-security sites, such as military bases, to detect, monitor, and report on intruders. Their sensors and cameras, assisted by AI software, can detect unauthorized visitors, cellular devices, and license plates. They can venture into dangerous situations to investigate, for example, suspected bombs or toxic substances, and they can make video and audio recordings to help identify trespassers. While ASR's usually operate autonomously, a human operator can take control if a robot detects something that requires urgent intervention.

Drone patrols. Teams of drones can be used to provide an additional layer of security against intruders. They can give real-time intelligence and video recordings of an intrusion in progress, and if the breach takes place at night, they can provide light illumination and thermal (heat) imaging to help security guards locate and identify the intruder. In the future, they may even be used to launch attacks against unauthorized drone incursions.

ENGAGE YOUR READER

Nonfiction writing often includes subject-specific vocabulary terms. Knowing the words related to the topic helps us understand the text itself.

When good readers come upon words they don't know well, they pause and try to figure them out. One tool they use is the glossary, like the one on page 4. Not every word can be defined in a glossary, though!

Authors know this, so they leave clues about words in the text. Next time you encounter a challenging word, stop and look for information about its meaning in the surrounding sentences. Sometimes authors define the term right there in the text! Other times, they'll compare the term to something you may already know. Authors even use punctuation like commas or dashes to clue you in to a word's meaning.

INSTRUCTIONS

1. Consider the list of challenge words and identify where each is used in the text. You can use the Index on page 48 to help you locate each term.

2. Explain how the author described each word. Ask yourself "what is happening in the text?" or "how is this word being used?" as you search for clues about their meanings.

3. Create your own definitions of the words. Don't just copy the dictionary definitions. Instead think about how you would tell a friend what each term means.

4. Add a visual representation for each word. Think about what you could draw that will help you remember what the words mean.

Visit www.worldbook.com/resources to download
your own graphic organizer as well as other free resources!

CHALLENGE WORDS

- Algorithm
- Biometric
- Data
- Identity
- Cybersecurity
- Sensor
- Surveillance
- Malware

EXAMPLE

Challenge Word	Page(s)	Author's Description	Personal Definition	Visual Representation
Algorithm	8-11, 14-19, 24-26, 34-35	- a set of rules that a computer can understand - computer program - instructions - software	An algorithm is a written set of rules that tell a computer what to do.	(flowchart diagram)
Biometric				

INDEX

A
access control, 15, 18, 36-45
antivirus software, 25
apps, 7, 34, 37, 39, 40, 41
artificial intelligence (AI) algorithms, 8, 9, 10, 11, 14, 15, 16, 17, 18, 19, 24, 25, 26, 27, 29, 30, 34, 35, 37, 43

B
banks, 7, 16, 18, 19, 23, 32
behavioral biometrics, 13, 18-19, 24
biometrics, 12-19, 24, 30, 39
body odor recognition, 15
botnets, 22
bots, 25

C
cameras, 9, 11, 18, 29, 30-31, 32, 34, 35, 44, 45
cloud-based servers, 21, 42
computer hacking, 21, 22, 34
computer viruses, 22
convolutional neural networks (CNN's), 8, 10-11
cybercrime, 21, 22-23, 24
cybersecurity, 20-27, 43

D
distributed denial-of-service (DDoS) attacks, 22, 24
door controllers, 38, 39, 40
drones, 30, 31, 35, 44, 45

E
emails, 22, 23
encryption, 21, 23, 24, 26, 27

F
faceprints, 8, 9, 13
facial emotion recognition (FER), 10-11
facial recognition, 6-11, 14, 30, 37, 39, 40
fingerprints, 7, 8, 13, 14, 37, 39, 40
firewalls, 24, 25

G
gait analysis, 13, 18
geofencing, 44

H
heartbeat recognition, 13, 15, 33

I
infrared cameras, 32
intercom systems, 39
internet, 21, 22, 24, 25, 29, 34, 39, 42, 44
Internet of Things, 21, 29, 37
intruders, 32, 33, 40, 44-45
iris recognition, 13, 14, 39, 40

K
keycards and fobs, 39, 40, 41, 43
keypads, 38, 39, 40

L
license plate recognition, 30, 35, 45
lockdowns, 38, 41

M
malware, 22, 23, 25, 27
micro aerial vehicles (MAV's), 31
motion sensors, 32
multifactor authentication (MFA), 40
multispectral imaging (MSI), 14

P
passwords, 13, 22, 23, 34, 40, 41
personal data, 21, 22, 23, 29, 34, 35
phishing, 23, 25
physical biometrics, 13, 14-15
police, 7, 9, 11, 13, 16, 34, 35, 39
privacy concerns, 9, 15, 19, 29, 32, 34

Q
quantum computing, 26-27
quantum key distribution (QKD), 27

R
radio frequency identification (RFID), 33, 39, 44
ransomware, 23
readers, 38, 39, 40, 41
robot security, 37, 45

S
security cameras, 9, 11, 18, 29, 30, 34, 35
sensors, 15, 18, 29, 30, 32-33, 35, 43, 45
smart buildings, 37, 43
smart dust, 33
smartphones, 7, 15, 29, 34, 37, 39, 40, 41, 42
software applications, 21, 22, 24, 42
spectrograms, 16
spyware, 22
surveillance, 28-35

T
telecommunications interceptions, 35
3D motion detection cameras, 30
touchless access control, 40
Trojan horses, 22

V
virtual assistants, 34
virtual reality (VR) helmets, 31
voice biometrics, 13, 14, 16-17, 34, 37, 39, 40
voice cloning, 17
voiceprints, 16, 17

W
Wi-Fi, 33, 41, 44
wipers, 22

www.ingramcontent.com/pod-product-compliance
Lightning Source LLC
Chambersburg PA
CBHW041138170426
43198CB00023B/2983